P9-DEV-376

DISCARDED

New Action Sports

BMX Bicycles

by Barbara Knox

CAPSTONE PRESS

MANKATO

C A P S T O N E   P R E S S

818 North Willow Street ● Mankato, MN 56001

Copyright © 1996 Capstone Press. All rights reserved. No part of this book may be reproduced in any form without written permission from the publisher.

Printed in the United States of America.

Library of Congress Cataloging-in-Publication Data
Knox, Barbara.
    BMX bicycles / Barbara Knox.
    p. cm.
    Includes bibliographical references and index.
    Summary: Describes the bicycles used in BMX racing, the techniques of riding, and various types of races.
    ISBN 1-56065-369-8 (hc)
    ISBN 0-7368-8082-8 (pb)
    1. Bicycle motocross--Juvenile literature. 2. Bicycles--Juvenile literature. [1. Bicycle motocross. 2. Bicycle racing.] I. Title.
GV1049.3.K56 1996
796.6'2--dc20

                                        95-44717
                                          CIP
                                          AC

Photo credits
Peter Ford: pp. 4, 6, 8, 10, 12, 13, 18, 20, 23,
  25, 26, 38, 40, 42
Charles W. Melton: pp. 14, 17, 32, 34, 35, 37, 45
Gork/ABA: p. 29, 30, 46

Chapter 1
BMX

BMX stands for bicycle motocross. BMX bikes are small and tough. They are built to fly over dirt jumps and race around tracks. BMX bike riding is an exciting sport enjoyed around the world.

At organized tracks, boys and girls as young as three years old compete for trophies and prizes. Many young people get together and build their own tracks in parks or vacant fields.

BMX bikes are small and tough.

Many young people build their own BMX tracks.

They meet and race for fun after school or on weekends.

Some BMXers like to do tricks on their bikes. This kind of riding is called **freestyle** BMX. It is easy to learn to race BMX or do tricks at home. All it takes is practice.

Once you learn the basics, you can decide for yourself if you want to race or do freestyle BMX. A lot of young riders do both. But you have to be prepared to take some falls. You will get some bruises while you learn.

The First BMXers

The idea to race and do tricks on bikes came from the 1970 movie *On Any Sunday*. It showed motorcycles flying through the air and bouncing across rough fields.

People tried to do the same kind of tricks on their bicycles at home. But their regular bikes could not take the pounding.

Bicycle manufacturers responded by making smaller bikes. These new bikes had very strong **frames** and small, sturdy tires. They were built for speed. They were also tough enough to jump over dirt mounds.

BMX has come a long way since 1970. Today, BMXers can choose from many different styles of bikes.

Table of Contents

Words in **boldface** type in the text are defined
in the Glossary in the back of this book.

Chapter 2

The Bikes

BMX bikes are single-speed bikes. They are different from street bikes. Most street bikes have 24- to 27-inch (61- to 69-centimeter) wheels. BMX bikes have 20-inch (51-centimeter) wheels.

There are some smaller, 16-inch (41-centimeter) BMX bikes made for young riders. These are called minis. Older riders often move on to 24-inch (61-centimeter) bikes. These are called cruisers. Minis and cruisers race in separate classes at organized events.

BMXers can choose from many different styles of bikes.

BMX bikes are made out of aluminum **alloy** or **chrome-moly**. Racers prefer the alloy because it is lighter. Lighter bikes are faster bikes. Freestylers prefer chrome-moly. It is heavier and stronger than the alloy.

Both styles of BMX bike start with the same basic frame.

Racers prefer aluminum alloy wheels.

The Frame Set

When you buy a BMX bike, you are buying a frame and a **fork**. Together they are called a frame set.

The frame is a triangle made up of three lightweight tubes welded together. They are the top tube, the down tube, and the seat tube. They support the rest of the bike.

The front fork is also made of tubes. The front wheel attaches to the front fork. The front fork takes most of the shock of hard riding. It has to be strong.

The Rear Triangle

The rear triangle is the back part of the bike. It includes the seat stays and the chain stays.

Stays are small metal tubes. Every bike has two seat stays and two chain stays. Together, these stays hold the rear wheel. The stays are welded to the frame.

The rear wheel fits into **drop-outs** where the stays come together. The drop-outs allow BMXers to change their wheel quickly and easily.

The pedals and the crank drive the chain and sprocket.

The Crank

Bike pedals attach to a metal piece called a **crank**. The pedals and the crank work together to drive the chain and sprockets. There are one-piece cranks and three-piece cranks.

One-piece cranks are the most common. Experienced BMX riders usually choose the more expensive three-piece cranks. Three-piece cranks are made of two arms connected by a **spindle**.

The Wheels

Wheels include the hub, the spokes, and the rim. There are two kinds of wheels. They are mag wheels and spoked wheels. Mag wheels have three to six main spokes made of molded plastic. Most BMXers use regular spoked wheels.

Racers use knobby tires.

Racers usually prefer aluminum-alloy wheels with 36 spokes. These wheels are light and strong. They do not slow the rider down with extra weight.

Freestylers usually prefer chrome-moly wheels with 48 spokes. These wheels are very strong. They can take the pounding that comes with freestyle riding.

The wheels should always spin freely between the stays. To check them, turn the bike upside down and spin the wheels. If a wheel wobbles, check the rim to see if it is bent.

Check the spokes by plucking them like guitar strings. If they feel loose or sound dull, they need to be tightened. Use a special spoke wrench. After a while, you will learn how tight to set the spokes. You will get a feel for it.

Freestylers prefer chrome-moly wheels.

Lincoln School Library
LaPorte, Indiana

The Tires

Racers use knobby tires with deep tread. For the best traction, they often put a slightly wider tire in front. Tire width varies between 1.5 and 2.125 inches (3.8 and 5.4 centimeters).

Younger racers do not need their tires to be as wide as tires needed by older, heavier riders. Racers are always trying to find a tire that gives them the traction they need but does not slow them down.

Narrower tires give the rider more speed. Freestylers do not need to go fast to do their tricks. They tend to use heavy street tires with a smooth tread.

The Brakes

Racing bikes have brakes on the rear wheel only. This keeps the bike's weight low.

Front brakes can be dangerous when used at top speeds. Sudden braking on the front wheel can cause the back of the bike to flip over the front. Then the rider would be thrown over the handlebars.

The gyro is located at the base of the handlebars.

Freestyle bikes have both front and rear brakes. Usually, there is a **caliper** brake on the rear wheel.

Sometimes, though, riders choose a free coaster brake. These keep the pedals in one place while the bike rolls backwards. They are great for some tricks.

The Gyro and Pegs

The **gyro** is the part that makes freestyle bikes different from racing bikes. It is located

Pegs are steel tubes attached to the axle.

at the base of the handlebars. It allows the freestyler to spin the handlebars all the way around. The gyro is key to most tricks that freestylers do.

Pegs are the steel tubes attached to the axle on both sides of the wheels. Pegs are found only on freestyle bikes. Freestylers stand on the pegs to do tricks.

The Chain

Bike chains should be tight. They should only move up and down about one-half inch (1.27 centimeters). You can change how tight the chain is by moving the rear wheel backward or forward.

Chains should be cleaned and oiled regularly. Most riders use something simple like a toothbrush and a standard cleaning fluid to clean their chains.

Other Parts

Sprockets are metal wheels with teeth. They hold the chain. BMX bikes have a large sprocket in the front and a smaller sprocket in the rear.

Pedals are made of steel or plastic. They have small teeth to grip the rider's shoe. Pedals need to be oiled to keep them spinning freely.

There are different types of seats. Racers choose unpadded seats to keep the bike's weight down. BMXers who just ride around every day will probably want padded seats. They are more comfortable. Always make sure that your seat is set at the right height for you.

Chapter 3
Safety

For every successful freestyle trick, you will probably take a hundred falls. For every racer who wins a **moto**, there are endless crashes and bruises.

Falling and crashing are part of BMX riding. Few riders, though, get seriously hurt.

Protection for the Rider

Almost all BMX racetracks are supervised by the American Bicycle Association (ABA). ABA officials require all racers to wear

There are full-face helmets and open-face helmets.

helmets, long sleeves, and long pants. Extra safety gear is optional.

Helmets

Bikers wear full-face helmets or open-face helmets. Full-face helmets have guards that cover the entire face and head. Open-face helmets only cover the head. Riders sometimes wear mouth guards with open-face helmets.

A good basic helmet is made of fiberglass. It has a padded liner that fits securely on your head. A chin strap holds the helmet in place. The chin strap should always be fastened while riding.

Helmets are expensive, so many ABA tracks lend helmets to the riders. Beginning riders who are not sure whether or not they like BMX racing can borrow a helmet for a day. They will not have to buy one until they are sure they want to keep riding.

Clothing

Most racers wear jeans and long-sleeved shirts. Some riders wear padded pants and shirts called leathers. They are made of strong

BMXers wear clothing made of strong fabrics.

fabrics. They have pads built into the hips, knees, and shins. The pants have narrow legs so they will not get caught in the bike chains.

Riders can buy shin guards, knee pads, and elbow pads to wear over their regular clothes. This extra protection is never wasted. Even professional BMX riders take frequent falls. Every BMX bike should have safety pads on the top tube, the stem, and the cross brace. Most BMX bikes come with these pads.

Gloves are not required, but many BMXers use them to get a better grip on the handlebars. Whether bikers are racing or doing tricks, keeping a firm grip is important.

Goggles and Shoes

BMX bikes kick up a lot of dirt, so racers often wear goggles. They protect racers' eyes and help them see clearly by keeping the dust out of their eyes.

Most BMXers wear high-top canvas shoes. High-tops help protect ankles from scrapes and cuts. Shoes should have soft soles to grip the pedals. There are shoes made just for riding BMX bikes. But most riders still wear common basketball or running shoes.

Some riders wear padded pants and shirts called leathers.

Chapter 4

BMX Racing

Some communities have indoor and outdoor tracks for BMX racing. More often, though, riders get together and build their own track in a park or field. They set their own rules and award their own prizes to the winners.

Join Up

If you plan to race regularly, you should join the American Bicycle Association, the National Bicycle League, or the Canadian BMX Association. The largest of these groups is the ABA.

Racers are grouped according to age and skill.

Membership in the ABA allows you to ride at the many official ABA tracks across North America. The ABA **insures** every rider who is a member of the organization.

When you join the ABA, they send you an official number plate. This is the number attached to your bike's handlebars for every race. You keep the same number for the entire racing season.

The ABA also keeps track of your points during the racing season. Racers want the fewest number of points possible. First-place winners are awarded one point. Second place gets two points. And so on.

At the end of the season, the racer with the fewest points will get the number one plate for next year's season. Second place will get number two. And so on.

Race Day

Racers are grouped according to age and skill. The youngest class is for racers five years old and under. The oldest class is for racers 19

A skilled rider takes a hill.

years old and over. Be prepared to show proof of your age at the track.

Track officials inspect all bikes before the race. They want to be sure there are no unsafe bikes. They also inspect safety gear. They check to see that every racer is wearing a helmet, a long-sleeved shirt, and long pants.

Two racers stay close on an indoor track.

Races are called motos. The pace is fast. Many motos are over in just 35 seconds. Racers start by riding in qualifying **heats**. Winners of the qualifying heats go to the main races. Winners of the main races win trophies or other prizes.

The Track

Most BMX races begin at a starting gate at the top of a hill. Along the track are banked turns called berms. The track might also include a banzai. This is a big hole in the ground. Riders land inside the banzais and then jump out.

Rounded dirt bumps placed close together on the track were called whoops, whoopties, or whoop-de-doos. Today, they are often called the rhythm section of the track.

The basic rhythm section is a series of six large bumps in a row. This is called a six-pack. Riders jump one or two bumps at a time. Some tracks might have seven-packs or eight-packs. A 12-pack is the longest series of jumps ever built into a track.

Sometimes the track includes a tabletop. This is a flat section of packed dirt in the middle of the whoopties. Different combinations in the rhythm section keep the race interesting.

Step-up and step-down jumps are also common on a racetrack. These jumps are like big stairsteps.

The best way to prepare for racing is to ride your bike a lot. Serious BMXers spend as much time as possible on their bikes. They practice with friends or by themselves.

Chapter 5

Freestyling

Freestyling was enormously popular in the mid-1980s. At that time, there were organized freestyle competitions all over North America.

Today, freestyling has gone back to being an individual sport. It is a great way for riders to have fun in their own driveway. Riders compete against themselves. They practice new tricks.

Professional freestylers offer great entertainment. Some groups perform around the country. They even do half-time shows at

Serious BMXers spend as much time as possible on their bikes.

Riders have to be willing to work hard.

basketball games and other professional sporting events.

Flatland

Most riders start freestyling by doing flatland tricks. These are mostly balancing tricks. The rider stands on the back pegs.

Flatland tricks take a lot of practice. Riders have to be strong and willing to work hard.

Box Jumping

Sometimes riders build **box jumps** in their own backyards. Box jumps have a straight ramp on one side, a flat table in the middle, and a curved ramp on the other side.

Sometimes skate parks have box jumps. They usually set aside different times for skateboarders and freestyle BMXers to use the jumps.

The kick-out is a popular trick.

There are many tricks you can do on box jumps. The kick-out is a popular trick. In a kick-out, riders jump into the air with both feet on the bike. Then they kick the back end of the bike out behind them in midair.

Ramps

Ramps are bigger than box jumps. They are more expensive to build, but many BMXers have built them anyway. Mini ramps are about five to seven feet (1.5 to two meters) tall.

Vertical ramps, or half-pipes, are about 10 to 12 feet (three to 3.6 meters) tall. These ramps are shaped like a wide U. They look like a giant pipe cut in half.

It is common to see these ramps in skateboard parks throughout North America. Most of them allow BMXers to practice tricks there, too.

Ramps look like a giant pipe cut in half.

Most BMXers build their own dirt jumps.

Dirt Jumps

Dirt jumping is something almost every BMXer enjoys. It is the common bond between racers and freestylers.

Most BMXers build their own dirt jumps. They bring shovels to a field and build a dirt hill about five feet (1.5 meters) high. The dirt hill is packed hard.

It is best if the dirt jump is at the bottom of a slight hill. Then riders can gain speed before they hit the jump.

Street Riding

Street freestyling is dangerous. Any BMXer who starts freestyling will hear about street tricks. In the street, riders slide along walls on their pegs. They do rail slides along public railings.

Street tricks can get you into trouble. They can get you hurt. Street tricks might sound exciting, but even good freestylers advise young riders to stay away from them.

Let's Go!

Racing or freestyling can be fun for riders of all ages. When you get your first BMX bike and start riding, you can learn about hundreds of different freestyle tricks. You can also learn dozens of racing techniques.

It all begins when you hop on a bike and get started.

Glossary

alloy–two or more metals mixed together

box jump–special kind of ramp used for freestyle tricks

caliper–U-shaped brake with rubber pads that press against the wheel

chrome-moly–very strong mixture of steel

crank–the metal arm to which the pedals are attached

drop-outs–flat metal pieces with slots welded to the stays

fork–part of the bike that holds the front tire

frame–main part of a bike, shaped like a triangle

Dirt jumping is something almost every BMXer enjoys.

freestyle—trick riding

gyro—bicycle part that allows riders to spin their handlebars all the way around

heat—preliminary round of a race

insure—to pay money for an insurance policy in case of injury or death

knobby tires—kind of tire that provides good traction

moto—BMX race on a track

spindle—small shaft that serves as an axis

There are hundreds of different freestyle tricks.

To Learn More

Brimner, Larry Dane. *BMX Freestyle.* New York: Franklin Watts, 1987.

Carstenson, Karol. *BMX Bikes.* Minneapolis: Capstone Press, 1991.

Gutman, Bill. *BMX Racing.* Minneapolis: Capstone Press, 1995.

Jay, Michael. *BMX Bikes.* New York: Franklin Watts, 1985.

Stephen, R. J. *The Picture World of BMX.* New York: Franklin Watts, 1989.

You can read articles about BMX riding in *BMX Plus Magazine*, *BMXer*, and *SNAP*.

Useful Addresses

American Bicycle Association
P.O. Box 718
Chandler, AZ 85244

Canadian BMX Association
1704 43rd Street
Vernon, BC V1T 6W8
Canada

United States Cycling Federation
c/o United States Olympic Committee
1750 East Boulder Street
Colorado Springs, CO 80909

U.S. Professional Cycling Federation
Route 1, Box 1650
New Tripoli, PA 18066

Index